Descriptosaurus Punctuation in Action Captain Moody and His Pirate Crew

Captain Christopher Moody, based on a real-life pirate, has always longed for adventure. So, when he finds a treasure map, he decides to find a crew, find the treasure and find the greatest adventure the world has ever seen! Meet some weird pirates, a spooky island and a fearsome sea monster in this epic tale.

On his journey, Captain Moody writes the story with the assistance of Blackbeard the pirate and Punctua, the Fairy Godmother of Writing, to punctuate properly and become a bestselling author.

Descriptosaurus Punctuation in Action Year 2: Captain Moody and His Pirate Crew is part of a short series of age-specific, beautifully illustrated stories that can be read for pleasure and/or used as a contextualised resource, containing a step-by-step guide to teaching punctuation. The characters from each story are used to demonstrate a range of punctuation rules in a fun and engaging way appropriate to the book's age group. Areas covered include:

- ★ formulating punctuation rules.
- ★ the use of misconceptions to highlight common errors.
- ★ teaching tips to provide a punctuation model.

The book explores the impact of punctuation on reading, understanding, meaning and effect, and can be used as a basis for pupils' own punctuation or included in their 'Writer's Toolkit.' These new *Descriptosaurus* stories are an indispensable teaching aid for making punctuation fun for all primary teachers and literacy coordinators.

Adam Bushnell is an award-winning and Amazon number one best-selling author of fictional and academic books. He works in the UK and internationally in both state and private education delivering creative writing workshops to all ages. His books have been selected by the School Library Association for the "Boys into Books" recommended reading list. Previously a teacher, Adam also delivers CPD to teachers and others working in education on how to inspire writing in the classroom.

Descriptosaurus Punctuation in Action Year 2

Captain Moody and His Pirate Crew

Adam Bushnell

Routledge
Taylor & Francis Group

LONDON AND NEW YORK

First published 2022
by Routledge
2 Park Square, Milton Park, Abingdon, Oxon OX14 4RN

and by Routledge
605 Third Avenue, New York, NY 10158

Routledge is an imprint of the Taylor & Francis Group, an informa business

© 2022 Adam Bushnell

British Library Cataloguing-in-Publication Data
A catalogue record for this book is available from the British Library

Library of Congress Cataloging-in-Publication Data
Names: Bushnell, Adam, author.
Title: Descriptosaurus punctuation in action year 2: Captain Moody and his pirate crew / Adam Bushnell.
Description: Abingdon, Oxon; New York, NY: Routledge, 2022. | Identifiers: LCCN 2021008204 | ISBN 9781032040783 (hardback) | ISBN 9781032040790 (paperback) | ISBN 9781003190431 (ebook)
Subjects: LCSH: English language–Punctuation–Juvenile literature.
Classification: LCC PE1450 .B87 2022 | DDC 428.2/3–dc23
LC record available at https://lccn.loc.gov/2021008204

ISBN: 9781032040783 (hbk)
ISBN: 9781032040790 (pbk)
ISBN: 9781003190431 (ebk)

DOI: 10.4324/9781003190431

Typeset in Myriad Pro
by Deanta Global Publishing Services, Chennai, India
Printed and bound by CPI Group (UK) Ltd, Croydon, CR0 4YY

Contents

Dedication and acknowledgement

For my friends and my family for all of their continued support.

Thanks also to the wonderful creator of the *Descriptosaurus* series, Alison Wilcox. She has been my guide, my teacher and my source of inspiration.

A big thanks to Bruce Roberts and Molly Selby of Routledge for their encouragement and guidance.

Huge thanks to the amazing and talented illustrators Nigel Clifton and Dani Pasteau for their contribution to this book.

Introduction

Research has demonstrated the negative impact SPAG (spelling, punctuation and grammar) has had on creativity. It has also revealed that the knowledge and application required in the context of the test have not resulted in a marked improvement in the quality of pupils' written texts as it is decontextualised and places emphasis primarily on identification and labelling. It does not, therefore, equip young writers to apply their knowledge of punctuation in their own writing, or, more specifically, assist them in developing a system for editing their own texts. In response, the new Ofsted Framework has focused on being able to demonstrate pupil progress in the writing process, which includes pupils being able to revise and edit their own written work.

Resources are, therefore, required to demonstrate models and support pupils with understanding the editing process, as well as developing their knowledge of writing conventions. In addition to providing models in the context of a short story, there is a need for young writers to be able to investigate, discuss and explore texts to assess the impact of punctuation on the reading and understanding of a text.

Whilst most punctuation resources provide models, it is a useful exercise for pupils to be presented with incorrect punctuation so that they can begin to understand the importance of communicating a clear meaning and can use that knowledge and understanding when editing their own texts. Each of the punctuation sections in these short stories will examine rules, misconceptions and common errors as well as providing punctuation models.

The *Descriptosaurus: Punctuation in Action* series are companion books to *Descriptosaurus Story Writing: Language in Action*, which was designed to combine the need to develop descriptive vocabulary for a wide range of settings and characters with models of story and sentence structure, and grammar, as well as exercises to scaffold pupils as they innovate and invent their own models. There are four stories in the series: *The Ninjabread Girl, Captain Moody and His Pirate Crew, Ruby Red* and *Jack and the Crystal Fang*. Each story has been written in a different style and with the curriculum needs of each year group in mind. The individual stories can be used, innovated and deconstructed according to the level, experience and knowledge of each age group, class or individual.

The story of *Captain Moody and His Pirate Crew* can be used for "reading for pleasure" but also contains a section on punctuation. The aim is to demonstrate punctuation in the context of a story and with characters that will have become familiar from reading the story. The characters are used to demonstrate a range of punctuation rules appropriate to the targeted age group:

1. formulating punctuation rules
2. using misconceptions to highlight common errors
3. using teaching tips to provide a punctuation model

They can be used as a basis for pupils' own punctuation posters and cards, or copied to include in their 'Writer's Toolkit.'

CAPTAIN MOODY AND HIS PIRATE CREW

Part A: The story of Captain Moody and His Pirate Crew

Captain Christopher Moody was a real-life pirate. This story includes some true parts of this pirate's life such as the design of his flag but follows him on an imaginary adventure that includes treasure, monsters, a spooky island and lots of pirates. It's a rollercoaster of a rollicking ride across the sea and to a land far away.

Part B: Learning punctuation with the characters

Join Captain Moody on his journey as he writes the story of becoming a pirate, finding a crew and searching for treasure. With the help of Blackbeard and Punctua (the Fairy Godmother of Writing) he learns how to punctuate properly and become a bestselling author.

Part A
The story of Captain Moody and His Pirate Crew

1

The map

DOI: 10.4324/9781003190431-1

Chris had always longed for adventure. Ever since he was a boy, he had dreamed of being a knight. Or a superhero. Or a dragon trainer. Something that would make his life exciting.

Instead, he was a fisherman. Every day he would row in his little boat across the sea and send his line into the water. Then he would wait … and wait … and wait. It was so boring! Sometimes something exciting would happen, like he would catch a crab instead of a fish. Or even catch something unusual like an old boot.

One day, Chris had rowed his boat over the calm and still sea. He was sitting holding his fishing rod when he felt it catch on something. It was probably caught on a jagged rock. He pulled and pulled but the line was stuck. Chris was about to cut the line with his penknife when he fell backwards.

"Ooof!"

He sat back up and reeled in the line. There, right on the end of his hook, was a bottle. It was old and dirty with a wooden stopper in the top. Chris pulled it free with a loud popping sound. He peered inside. There was rolled-up piece of paper. With slightly shaking hands, Chris pulled it out. He uncurled the paper and stared at it.

The Forest of Doom was marked on there. So was the Volcano of Death. There were other places too: the Swamp of Stink, the River of Evil, the Waterfall of Terror, the Lake of Madness and finally the Cave of Monsters. Right next to this last place was a bright red X.

Chris stood up quickly, making the boat wobble. He had a treasure map! He decided right then and there to become not a knight or a superhero or a dragon trainer but instead a … pirate!

"Yar!" he said, as he thought that was what a pirate might have said.

2

The crew

DOI: 10.4324/9781003190431-2

Chris rowed the boat back to the harbour as fast as he could. His mind was racing. He wouldn't just be any pirate. He would be the captain. He had the map after all. He needed new smart clothes, as captains always seemed to dress quite nicely. He needed a tricorn hat to show he was the boss. He needed a cutlass and a flintlock pistol as he wouldn't take any nonsense from his crew. Crew! Where would he find a crew? Where would he find a ship?

As his boat was tied to the pier, Chris saw a huge ship approaching the harbour. It had the figurehead of a pirate and the familiar black flag with a skull and crossed bones.

"Pirates!" Chris gasped.

He sprinted to the tailor's and bought a new jacket and hat, then raced to the blacksmiths for a sword and a gun. Once fully dressed as a pirate captain he ran back to the harbour.

Chris suddenly stopped. The ship had docked and the pirates on board were all carrying their captain.

"Call yourself a captain?" one pirate roared, "You haven't found us any treasure for ages!"

"Throw him in the sea!" another bellowed, "Feed him to the sharks!"

"Get rid of him!" a third cried, "We need a new captain!"

Chris stopped. He watched the unfortunate pirate captain land with a mighty splash in the water. He then swam wildly away from the ship and the other pirates as fast as he could.

Chris gulped and walked slowly toward the ship.

"Ahoy there!" he cried, feeling that he was really getting the hang of this pirate talk, "If you need a new captain, then I'm your man … Yar!"

The pirates on the ship looked at him as he approached. Chris gulped again.

3

The flag

DOI: 10.4324/9781003190431-3

"What's your name then?" one pirate asked.

"My name is Christopher Moody, but you can call me *Captain Moody*!"

The pirates looked him up and down.

"Your clothes look brand new!" another commented, "What ships have you sailed on?"

"Erm … the *Good Ship Betty* … Yar!"

"Never heard of it," a third laughed, "What makes you think we'd be your crew?"

"Because I have this!"

Chris dramatically pulled the treasure map from his belt. The crew all stared at it wide-eyed.

"We're your crew!" they chorused together.

Chris beamed and asked,

"What be your names … Yar!"

"I'm Stinky Sid," one pirate replied.

"I'm Peg Leg Pete," another answered.

"I'm Mad Mary," a third cried.

The fourth member of the crew was lowering the ship's flag.

"I'm Tina Tailor and I'll make us a new flag!"

"Yeah, a better one than last time," Stinky Sid said, "Let's put stuff like unicorns, butterflies and kittens on this time."

The pirates all looked at him.

"No," Chris firmly said, "I want it to be as red as blood and covered in piratey things like skulls and swords!"

Tina Tailor went below deck to make the flag straight away. Chris had a crew and adventure was not far away.

4

The journey

DOI: 10.4324/9781003190431-4

Chris studied the map and pointed to the north. The red flag with a golden skull, white sword and blue hourglass timer flapped in the wind. The sky was darkening and the sea turned from blue to grey. Clouds gathered above like a flock of black sheep.

The island was not too far from the mainland. But Chris knew that with the approaching storm it was not going to be easy. Soon, waves were beating the sides of the ship. Rain lashed at them from above. The wind became a howling monster that lashed at them from all around.

Chris held tightly to the ship's wheel and tried to look brave. The other pirates clung on for dear life. Somehow, with lots of luck, and even more rum, they did it.

They were through the storm and saw the island on the horizon. The weather changed almost instantly. The sea was now calm and still. The clouds cleared into wisps of white fluff.

The ship sailed slowly into a shallow reef. The water here was emerald green. Rainbow-coloured fish darted between red, leafy coral.

"Gather around, crew!" Chris commanded.

The pirates closed in around the map.

"Let's park there at the top!" declared Chris, pointing at the Cave of Monsters with the red X.

"What?" cried the crew, clearly appalled.

"What's wrong?" asked Chris.

"You don't *park* a ship," growled Stinky Sid.

"You don't go straight to the X either!" snarled Peg Leg Pete.

"You have to go to each place first!" barked Mad Mary.

"That's the pirate way!" shouted Tina Tailor.

Chris shrugged and thought it best to just say, "Yar!"

5

The island

DOI: 10.4324/9781003190431-5

22 The island

The pirates dropped anchor to the south of the small tropical island. The beach was empty and the island looked deserted. The Forest of Doom was just beyond the beach. It was wild and overgrown. That would be their first stop.

They lowered a boat into the water and Stinky Sid rowed the crew to the beach. The golden beach had powdery white sand. The pirates followed Chris as he passed palm trees with huge leaves like a fan.

The Forest of Doom was a terrifying place. The moment the crew entered they were freezing cold. Gone were the tropical waters, sandy beach and blazing sunshine. Instead, a cold wind crept through the forest. White human and animal bones were scattered all around. Skeletons, skulls and jawbones littered the forest floor.

A roaring sound in the distance made the trees shake slightly and the pirates shake even more.

"Erm, pirate crew?"

They grabbed hold of him.

"Yes, Captain?" they chorused together.

"So, this is the Forest of Doom. Then we need to go to the Volcano of Death, the Swamp of Stink, the River of Evil, the Waterfall of Terror, Tthe Lake of Madness and finally the Cave of Monsters."

The pirates all nodded.

"Or we could just park at the top of the island and go straight to the X."

The pirates all nodded even more.

Then they were off. The crew raced back to the golden sandy beach and leapt into the rowboat. Stinky Sid rowed over a stunning, rainbow-coloured coral reef that lay beneath the surface of the water. Then they climbed a rope ladder, back to the safety of the ship.

6

The monster

DOI: 10.4324/9781003190431-6

The Cave of Monsters was at the northern tip of the island. Here high rocks rose vertically out of the sea. Chris had to carefully steer the ship to drop anchor. Stinky Sid rowed the boat slowly past huge, jagged rocks that guarded the island. The grey tip of a shark's fin sliced through the water nearby.

Eventually, they made it to the shore. The beach here was scattered with objects from an ancient shipwreck. The battered remains of ships were strewn about here and there.

The cave was ahead of them. According to the map, the treasure chest was buried under rocks just inside the cave. Chris stepped forward and peered at the cave's entrance. A skeleton of an enormous creature blocked the mouth of the cave. The bones were bleached white from the sun.

"Maybe this is the monster?" Stinky Sid said, uncertainly.

"So, it's dead!" grinned Peg Leg Pete.

"Let's just go in and get the treasure then!" smiled Mad Mary.

"Isn't it the Cave of Monsters?" asked Tina Tailor, "As in plural?"

Chris drew his cutlass just at the moment the monster burst from the darkness of the cave. It had the head of a shark, tentacles of an octopus, shell of a turtle, claws of a lobster and tail of a stingray. It towered above the pirate crew and roared a terrible roar. It gnashed its teeth, snapped its claws and crawled towards them. The octopus tentacles coiled over every rock as it approached.

Chris and his crew turned to run back to the boat. But the monster leapt up into the air and landed with a splat on the beach. It blocked their way of escape. It was either run away or fight. Chris pulled free his flintlock pistol and watched his crew scream then run in terror.

They hid in the cave. Chris was on his own.

7

The battle

DOI: 10.4324/9781003190431-7

Chris held the sword in one hand and the gun in the other. His hands were shaking and his knees were knocking.

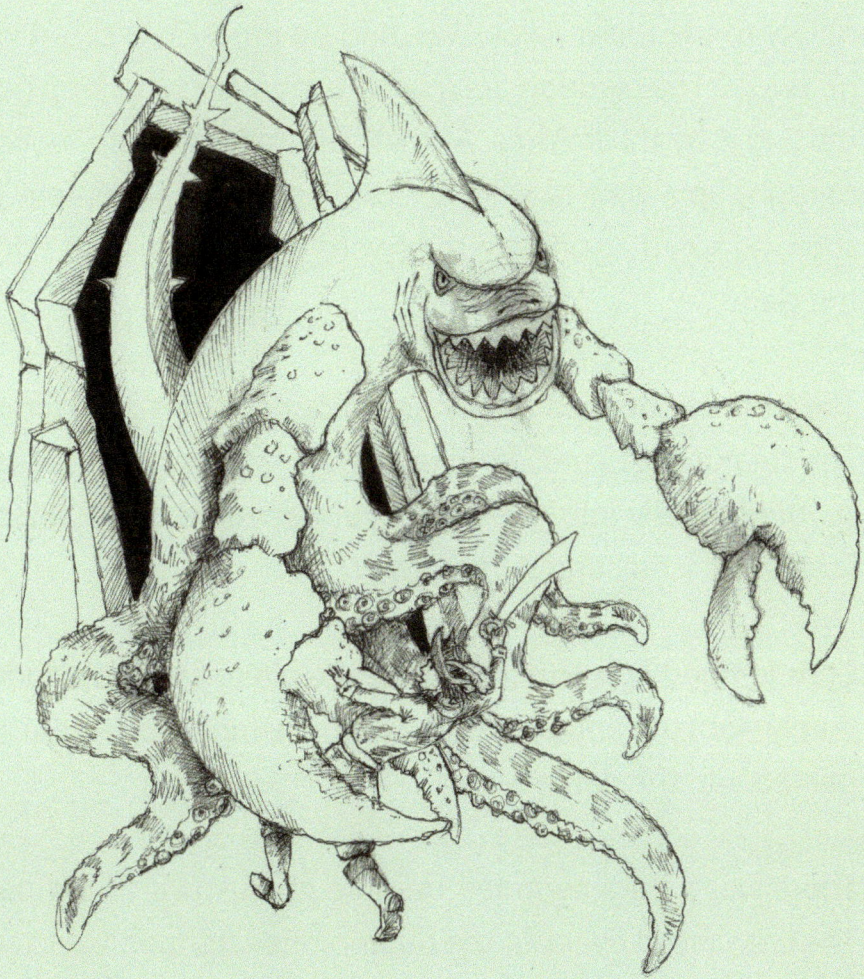

Suddenly, the monster roared again and began to creep towards him. Wasting no time, Chris aimed and shot his flint-lock pistol … and missed. Without warning, the creature stretched out a long, slithering tentacle and grabbed him. It brought him close to the snapping jaws that dripped saliva noisily to the rocks below. Wasting no time, Chris sliced with his sword. The blade swung past the monster's shark-tip nose, missing it by millimetres. At that very moment, the monster brought up a claw to snap at Chris' neck. Not a moment too soon, he sliced again with the sword and cut the hard skin of the claw.

The monster howled loudly and dropped Chris with a thud. The creature then held its injured claw with its other claw and scuttled rapidly into the water. It disappeared under the surface of the water and darted away.

Chris jumped up to his feet to see the pirate crew applauding madly from the entrance of the cave. He ran to join them and peered into the darkness.

There was a huge wooden treasure chest towards the back. The crew raced over but the other pirates stepped back to let their captain have the honour of opening it. The lid was carved with strange symbols. Chris lifted it slowly, then gasped.

Piles of jewels, sapphires, rubies and diamonds glittered from the bottom of the chest. The pirates cheered again.

"Let's get this to our ship before the monster gets back," Chris suggested.

"Aye aye, captain!" the pirates replied.

The four crew members grabbed a corner of the chest each and Chris led them down to the beach. He held out his cutlass menacingly all the while to warn off any monsters.

8

The party

DOI: 10.4324/9781003190431-8

With the treasure safely stowed aboard the ship, they were off. The ship sailed smoothly over the crystal-clear water. The sky was a beautiful blue and the sun shone happily above the pirate crew.

When they docked the ship at the harbour, the pirate crew had a party. Chris was now Captain Moody and he was the happiest he had ever been. They all ate until their bellies burst and drank until they were drowning. It was a pirate's dream brought to life!

Part B

Learning punctuation with the characters

9

Meet the characters

Section 1: Captain Moody

Section 2: Blackbeard

Section 3: Punctua (the Fairy Godmother
of Writing)

DOI: 10.4324/9781003190431-9

SECTION 1: CAPTAIN MOODY

Hi, I'm Captain Moody, the author of this story. I am delighted with the published story and hope you enjoyed reading it as much as I enjoyed writing it.

I want to say a huge thank you to Punctua, my fairy godmother. Without her assistance, I wouldn't have been able to turn my exciting ideas into a fabulous story that I hope you found easy to read, understand and enjoy.

Whilst Blackbeard was irritating, as he picked up all my mistakes, his comments were actually very useful for showing me that it is important to punctuate my writing correctly so that my readers can enjoy the story.

SECTION 2: BLACKBEARD

Blackbeard refused to give an interview, but issued the following statement:

Captain Moody left the first draft of his story in a bottle floating in the sea. I only managed the first page, and that took me ages to read. My first thought was, "This pirate should spend less time looking for treasure and more time in the classroom." However, I admit that now he has learned how to edit it correctly, it is a good, well-written story.

Blackbeard (the best pirate in the world)

SECTION 3: PUNCTUA (THE FAIRY GODMOTHER OF WRITING)

Greetings,
readers.
I'm Punctua,
the Fairy
Godmother of Writing. I
have worked with all the famous
authors over many centuries.

Captain Moody was a delight to work
with. His ideas were brilliant, and he
was keen to learn how to make them
clear, exciting and easy to read
and understand.

He worked hard every day
learning about punctuation until
his story was edited correctly and ready
for publication and performance.
He thoroughly deserves all his
success. Well done, Captain
Moody, on becoming an
international bestsell-
ing author.

Punctua

10

Editing a story

Section 1: Writing and editing tips

Section 2: Sentences

Section 3: Comma splicing

DOI: 10.4324/9781003190431-10

CAPTAIN MOODY'S WRITING TIPS:

When I have a really good story to tell, the words in my head want to spill onto the page. But when I stop and start the story to check my spelling and punctuation, then I can't remember what I wanted to happen next.

The best way for me to write is to "spill" my story onto the page and when I have finished it, read it aloud, either to myself or to Punctua. This makes it easier to spot when it doesn't make sense and I need to insert punctuation marks.

Sometimes, Punctua reads it aloud to me. I can then easily hear where I need to include or change some of my punctuation marks.

To help me with my editing, I make little punctuation rule cards and include a number of examples.

Captain Christopher Moody

PUNCTUA'S POINTS:

When you are editing your writing, **read it aloud** and:

★ note when you **pause**.
★ put a pencil mark at that point in your text.

Ask:

★ Why did I **pause**?
★ Was it because:

    a. the thought, statement, idea or description was **complete**?
    b. you had to re-read what was written because it **didn't make any sense**?

CAPTAIN MOODY'S FIRST DRAFT:

my name is captain christopher moody and I went to an island to look for treasure

Editing a story

The first draft:

Read it aloud.

Does it make sense?

Start with checking the sentences for full stops and capital letters.

BLACKBEARD'S WHINES:

Yar! This makes no sense! They are *not* sentences.

I'm finding it too hard to read and understand.

PUNCTUA'S POINTS:

Punctuation is a series of traffic signals. Without it, words bang together, and your writing won't make any sense. It will take your reader a long time to get to the end and they could get terribly lost.

A **full stop** is the most important **punctuation mark**. It helps you to **signal to your reader** that the **sentence has ended**, and the statement (thought, description, idea) is **complete**.

When reading your first draft, ask yourself these questions:

1. Is this a sentence?
2. Does it make **sense**?
3. Is it **complete** or do extra words need to be added?
4. Does it start with a **capital letter** and end with a **full stop**?

In Captain Moody's first draft, there were no full stops or capital letters, and no complete sentences.

my name is captain christopher moody and I went to an island to look for treasure

1. We need a **capital letter** at the start – **M**y – and a **full stop** at the end.
2. Where is the first complete statement? My name is Captain Christopher Moody.
3. Where is the second complete statement? I went to an island to look for treasure.

Note: Captain Moody has joined the first two points with **and** to **combine them into one sentence**.

So, the first complete sentence should have been:

My name is Captain Christopher Moody and I went to an island to look for treasure.

There is a **capital letter** *at the start and a* **full stop** *at the end. The two sentences are* **joined** *together using* **and**.

SECTION 2: SENTENCES

Sentences

There are four types of sentences:

★ statement (.)
★ question (?)
★ command/instruction (.)
★ exclamation (!)

CAPTAIN MOODY'S RULES:

We dropped anchor when we reached the island. **(statement)**

Aye, aye, captain! **(exclamation)**

Is there more than one monster? **(question)**

Get the treasure on board the ship. **(command)**

BLACKBEARD'S WHINES:

But in Captain Moody's first draft he thought a sentence ended in a full stop, regardless of whether it was a statement, question or exclamation.

PUNCTUA'S POINTS:

Remember: punctuation marks are a series of traffic signals.

Punctuation marks make it **easier to read** and **understand what has been written** and **how** it is meant to be **read** or **spoken**.

(There are more tips about question marks and exclamation marks later.)

It is true to say that **every sentence ends with a full stop**.

Look closely at the **bottom** of a **question mark** and an **exclamation mark**. What do you notice?

Both have a full stop at the bottom!

Recap:

A **sentence** is a **unit of words** that is **complete** and **makes sense**.

It can be a **statement**, **question**, **exclamation** or **instruction**.

A **sentence** always **starts** with a **capital letter** and **ends** with a **full stop**.

SECTION 3: COMMA SPLICING

Comma splicing

★ Commas cannot be used to join two complete sentences.

★ Use a conjunction to join two sentences instead.

CAPTAIN MOODY'S RULES:

Sometimes two **sentences** link ideas, thoughts or descriptions and you want to join the sentences together.

A comma *cannot* be used to join two sentences. This is called **comma splicing**.

You need to use a **conjunction** to link the two sentences.

BLACKBEARD'S WHINES:

Yar! Sentence splicing can walk the plank. Sentence splicing can be fed to the sharks. I hate it! It is painful to read.

Captain Moody spliced so many sentences in his first draft, it was terrible. He wrote:

The monster roared, I was scared.

It was hard to get the treasure, I managed it though.

PUNCTUA'S POINTS:

For your writing to flow and not sound jerky, it is important to **vary the length of your sentences**.

But **two complete sentences cannot be joined by a comma**.

You need to use a **conjunction**, for example: **and**, **but**, **so.**

When editing your writing, *check*:

★   how many complete statements are included in one sentence?
★   have you joined them using a comma or a conjunction?

Examples:

We can link two sentences to:

1.   **add another statement** using **and**.

   The monster roared **and** I was scared.

2.   **add a different option** using **but**.

   It was hard to get the treasure **but** I managed it though.

11

Capital letters

Section 1: Beginning of a sentence and names of people

Section 2: Names of places

Section 3: Days of the week and months of the year

Section 4: Editing checklist

DOI: 10.4324/9781003190431-11

SECTION 1: BEGINNING OF A SENTENCE AND NAMES OF PEOPLE

Capital letters

★ start every sentence.
★ are used for names of people.

CAPTAIN MOODY'S RULES:

Capital letters are used:

★ to start a sentence.
★ for the names of people.
★ for 'I.'

Examples: My name is **C**hristopher **M**oody. **I** met the pirate crew including **S**tinky **S**id and **M**ad **M**ary.

BLACKBEARD'S WHINES:

In the first draft, there were no capital letters for the names of people. Captain Moody wrote **captain christopher moody**.

By the way, my real name is Edward Teach.

PUNCTUA'S POINTS:

Capital letters are **signposts** that help us to understand a text, spot the **characters** and **places** easily.

Captain Moody remembered to **start his sentences** with a capital letter, and he remembered a capital letter for '**I**.'

However, he forgot about the **names of people**.

Captain Moody and **Punctua** both start with a capital letter, as do **Edward Teach**, **Stinky Sid** and **Mad Mary**.

SECTION 2: NAMES OF PLACES

Capital letters

★ start every sentence.
★ are used for names of people and 'I.'
★ are used for names of places.

CAPTAIN MOODY'S RULES:

Capital letters are used for:

★ names of **places**.

Examples:

On the island were the **F**orest of **D**oom, the **V**olcano of **D**eath and the **S**wamp of **S**tink.

BLACKBEARD'S WHINES:

Captain Moody's first draft had no capital letters for places. He wrote:

I travelled to an island. On it was the forest of doom, the volcano of death, the swamp of stink, the river of evil, the waterfall of terror, the lake of madness and the cave of monsters.

How could I know that these were places without capital letters?

PUNCTUA'S POINTS:

Capital letters are **signposts** that help us to spot the **names of places** easily.

Captain Moody forgot that the **forest** has a name, as does the **volcano** and the names of all the other **places**.

He should have written:

I travelled to an island. On it was the **F**orest of **D**oom, the **V**olcano of **D**eath, the **S**wamp of **S**tink, the **R**iver of **E**vil, the **W**aterfall of **T**error, the **L**ake of **M**adness and the **C**ave of **M**onsters.

**SECTION 3: DAYS OF THE WEEK
AND MONTHS OF THE YEAR**

Capital Letters
1. start every sentence.
2. are used for:
   ★ names of people and 'I.'
   ★ names of places.
   ★ days of the week.
   ★ months of the year.

CAPTAIN MOODY'S RULES:

Capital letters are important.
They **start a sentence** and
should be used for:

a. names of **people**, as well as '**I**.'
b. names of **places**.
c. **days** of the week.
d. **months** of the year.

BLACKBEARD'S WHINES:

You scallywags keep forgetting …

★ days of the week.
★ months of the year.

It's Saturday, not saturday; January, not january.

PUNCTUA'S POINTS:

I gave this model for Captain Moody to keep in his **Writer's Toolkit**. Whenever
he can't remember when to use capital letters, he can use this **model** to help
him. It's always useful to have a model to look at when you are editing.

My name is **Captain Christopher Moody**. One
Saturday in **January**, I went on an adventure
with **Stinky Sid**, **Peg Leg Pete**, **Mad Mary** and
Tina Tailor. We travelled to an island. On it were
the **Forest of Doom**, the **Volcano of Death**, the
Swamp of Stink, the **River of Evil**, the **Waterfall
of Terror**, the **Lake of Madness** and the **Cave of
Monsters**.

SECTION 4: EDITING CHECKLIST

EDITING CHECKLIST:

I found it hard to remember where to put capital letters, so Punctua and I came up with this checklist to use when I am editing.

I take each item one at a time:

1. beginning of every sentence ☐
2. names of people ☐
3. 'I' ☐
4. names of places ☐
5. days of the week ☐
6. months of the year ☐

Capital letters

1. start every sentence.
2. are used for:
   ★ names of people, including 'I.'
   ★ names of places.
   ★ days of the week.
   ★ months of the year.

12

Question marks

DOI: 10.4324/9781003190431-12

Question marks

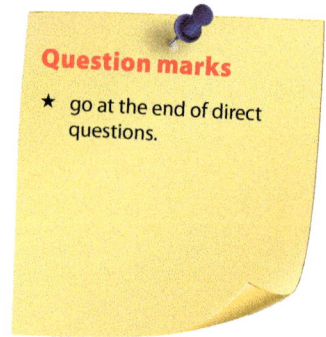

★ go at the end of direct questions.

CAPTAIN MOODY'S RULES:

Question marks go **at the end** of **direct questions**, which usually begin with words like:

Who? What? When?

Why? Where? How?

Is? Are? Can? Will?

BLACKBEARD'S WHINES:

Who is the greatest pirate that ever lived?

Who is the real captain here?

Who needs to ask for pirate lessons, but forgets to put question marks at the end of his questions?

PUNCTUA'S POINTS:

Young writers:

★ get **direct** and **indirect questions** confused.
★ forget the **question mark** at the **end of the sentence**.

Direct question:

★ where the speaker's **exact words are repeated**

For example:

What have you found**?** **Who** did you meet**?** **When** did you get the treasure**?**

Indirect question:

★ where the exact words are **not repeated**

For example:

The pirates **asked me** what I had found. Captain Blackbeard **asked me** who I had met.

13

Exclamation marks

DOI: 10.4324/9781003190431-13

Exclamation marks

Exclamation marks are used to show:

★ surprise.
★ an outburst.
★ humour.

CAPTAIN MOODY'S RULES:

Exclamation marks signal:

★ **surprise**: Oh! A monster is in the cave!
★ **an outburst**: Ow! Get those claws off me!
★ **humour**: What's a pirate's favourite robot?
  ARRR 2-D2!

BLACKBEARD'S WHINES:

Captain Moody has not been a captain for very long. He thinks you need to emphasise *everything*. So, he shouts and screams a lot. Even more than me!

In his first draft, he either forgot to signal a surprise or an outburst by using an exclamation mark, or he put exclamation marks at the end of *every* sentence, which is ridiculous.

PUNCTUA'S POINTS:

Exclamation marks are a **signal** to the reader that the **character** has a **strong emotional reaction** to something.

It could be:

★   a **surprise**.
★   an **outburst**.
★   a **joke**.

Example:

Oh**!** A monster is in the cave**!**

They are extremely useful for **emphasis** but should **not** be used **too often**.

14

Inverted commas (speech marks)

Section 1: When and how to use inverted commas

Section 2: How to punctuate inside the inverted commas

DOI: 10.4324/9781003190431-14

Inverted commas (speech marks)

Inverted commas (speech marks) are used to:

★ identify dialogue (direct speech).
★ enclose the exact words spoken.
★ Use commas to separate speech from the rest of the sentence.

CAPTAIN MOODY'S RULES:

★ Use **inverted commas** to **quote the exact words** someone has **said**.
★ Usually use **"double quotation marks"** (*66* and *99*).
★ Also called **speech marks**.

Example:

"I can hear the monster roaring from its cave."

★ **the exact words spoken by the pirates**
★ enclosed within **inverted commas** at the **beginning** and the **end**

BLACKBEARD'S WHINES:

In the first draft, Captain Moody wrote:

The pirate shouted from the beach I can hear the monster roaring in its cave.

I had difficulty working out what exactly the pirate had said.

At first, I thought he meant you could only hear the monster from the beach.

PUNCTUA'S POINTS:

1. The pirate shouted from the beach I can hear the monster roaring from its cave.

To ensure that the reader doesn't get confused about **who is talking** and **what they say**, we need to use **inverted commas** to **separate the speaker** and **their words**.

"I can hear the monster roaring in its cave." (This is what the pirate said.)

To **separate the speech from the rest of the sentence** and make it clear **what is being said by whom** we **need a comma**.

The pirate shouted from the beach**,** "I can hear the monster roaring in its cave."

We could have put the **speech first**, but we still need a **comma** to **separate the speech** and the **speaker**.

"I can hear the monster roaring in its cave**,**" the pirate shouted from the beach.

(Note: the comma comes inside the inverted commas.)

SECTION 2: HOW TO PUNCTUATE INSIDE THE INVERTED COMMAS

Inverted commas (speech marks)

The words a person says always begin with a capital letter.

★ Question marks and exclamation marks go inside the speech marks.

★ If the quotation ends a sentence, put a full stop before the closing speech marks.

★ Start a new line for each new speaker.

CAPTAIN MOODY'S RULES:

1. The words a person says always **begin** with a **capital letter**.

For example:

"**W**alk the plank," the pirate said. (The pirate said, "**W**alk the plank.")

2. The **question mark** or **exclamation mark** goes **inside the inverted commas**.

For example:

"Oh no**!**" I screamed. "What will the monster do**?**"

3. If the **speech ends a sentence**, a **full stop** goes **before the closing inverted commas**.

For example:

The pirate said**,** "I think we should leave**."**

4. Start a **new line** every time there is a **change** in the **person speaking**.

BLACKBEARD'S WHINES:

In the first draft, Captain Moody wrote:

"Oh no. What will the monster do," I asked, nervously. "I think we should leave".

PUNCTUA'S POINTS:

It can be very confusing for the reader if dialogue is not punctuated correctly.

Top tip:

> **Start** the speech using a **capital letter inside the opening inverted commas**.

> **End** the speech with a **comma**, **full stop**, **question mark** or **exclamation mark inside the closing inverted commas**.

Tricky bit:

When the quotation is **interrupted**, it can get a bit tricky. Look at the following examples:

"Oh no, what will the monster do**?**" I shrieked.

If we break this quotation up:

> "**O**h no**,**" I shrieked**,** "**w**hat will the monster do?"

Note: break up the speech using: (i) a **comma after the first words spoken**, (ii) **a comma after the speaker** and (iii) **no capital letter when the speech is restarted**.

15

Apostrophes

Section 1: Apostrophes for possession

Section 2: Apostrophes for contraction

DOI: 10.4324/9781003190431-15

SECTION 1: APOSTROPHES FOR POSSESSION

CAPTAIN MOODY'S RULES:

An apostrophe (') + s **shows possession**.

It shows that **something** is **owned** by **someone** or is **connected** to **something**.

For example:

The map belonging to the captain.

The captain**'s** map.

The compass belonging to the pirate.

The pirate**'s** compass.

BLACKBEARD'S WHINES:

In the first draft, Captain Moody wrote:

The monsters' claws.

Seems that he knew an apostrophe had to go somewhere *but* he didn't know *where*.

He also wrote:

"We are all pirates'."

PUNCTUA'S POINTS:

1. Monsters' claws

    There is only a **single** monster. The **claws belong** to **one monster**.

    Who **owns** the **claws**? The **monster**.

    Add **'s** to monster = **monster's**, *not* **monsters'**.

2. "We are all pirates'."

    Does anything **belong** to the pirates? **No**. No need for an apostrophe.

    "We are all **pirates**." (pirates is plural)

CAPTAIN MOODY'S RULES:

If something is owned by more than one person and the plural noun ends in 's':

For example:

The treasure belonging to the **pirates**.

pirate**s** ends in '**s**.'

Add an **apostrophe** after the 's.'

The **pirates'** treasure.

Apostrophes

★ Apostrophes are used to show possession.

★ For plural nouns ending in 's,' just add an apostrophe after the 's.'

BLACKBEARD'S WHINES:

In the first draft, Captain Moody wrote:

The pirate's swords clashed together.

The heroes's treasure was shared out.

PUNCTUA'S POINTS:

The pirate's swords.

There is **more than one** pirate.

The plural of pirate is **pirates**. It ends in '**s**'.

As it already ends in 's' just **add an apostrophe** after the '**s**'.

★   **the pirates' swords**

The heroes's treasure.

The treasure belonged to more than one hero.

The plural of hero is **heroes.**

It already ends in 's' – **add an apostrophe** after the '**s**'.

★   **heroes' treasure**

What if the **plural** noun **doesn't end in 's'**? For example, **children**.

You need to add **apostrophe and 's'**: **children's room**

CAPTAIN MOODY'S RULES:

If the something is owned by a **singular noun**, for example, **Hercules**, which ends in '**s**':

Example:

A club belonging to Hercules.

Hercules already ends in '**s**'.

Add an apostrophe after the '**s**'.

Example:

★ **Hercules' club**

BLACKBEARD'S WHINES:

In the first draft Captain Moody wrote:

Thoma's eyepatch.

Bes's compass.

PUNCTUA'S POINTS:

Example: Thoma's eyepatch

The eyepatch belongs to **Thomas**.

Thomas is **singular** and **ends in** '**s**'.

Add an **apostrophe after** '**s**'.

★ **Thomas' eyepatch**

Example: Bes's compass

The compass belongs to Bess.

Bess is **singular** and **ends in** '**s**'.

Add an **apostrophe after** '**s**'.

★ **Bess' compass**

SECTION 2: APOSTROPHES FOR CONTRACTION

MISSING!

> **Apostrophes: contractions**
>
> Apostrophes are used to show when two words have been joined together.
>
> ★ Some letters are missing.
> ★ Missing letters are replaced by an apostrophe.

CAPTAIN MOODY'S RULES:

Apostrophes are used to show where the missing letters go when **two words** have been **joined** and **shortened**.

For example:

I'm (I **a**m); you're (you **a**re); she's (she **i**s); it's (it **i**s);

they're (they **a**re); he'll (he **wi**ll); can't (can**no**t); don't (do n**o**t); there's (there **i**s)

BLACKBEARD'S WHINES:

Yar, me hearties! When Captain Moody edited his story, he still got **she's/shes** and **they're/there** mixed up and the wrong way round.

He wrote:

She is my best pirate. **Shes** with the other pirates. **There** on the pirate ship. Over **they're** on the other side of the island.

What do you think, Punctua?

PUNCTUA'S POINTS:

Example 1:

She's my best pirate. ✓

Shes my best pirate. (**no apostrophe**) ✗

Example 2:

They're on the pirate ship. ✓

There on the pirate ship. ✗

Example 3:

Over **there** on the other side of the island. ✓

Over **they're** on the other side of the island. ✗

Apostrophes:

Don't confuse:

★ she's/shes
★ they're/there

16

Commas

Section 1: In a list

Section 2: To avoid misunderstandings

Section 3: To separate parts of a sentence

DOI: 10.4324/9781003190431-16

SECTION 1: IN A LIST

SHOPPING LIST

CAPTAIN MOODY'S RULES:

Commas separate items in a list to make the meaning clear.

Instead of saying:

Sword **and** gun **and** map **and** hat **and** compass.

Replace **and** with a **comma** except for the last item in the list.

Sword**,** gun**,** map**,** hat **and** compass.

BLACKBEARD'S WHINES:

If you don't use **commas to separate items in a list**, it can be very confusing.

Cutlass sword flintlock pistol treasure map tricorn hat compass

Captain Moody couldn't understand the list and got:

Cutlass, sword flintlock, pistol treasure, map tricorn, hat compass.

Whatever some of those things are!

PUNCTUA'S POINTS:

Commas are needed to make the meaning of a **list** clear and avoid any misunderstandings.

A comma can be used instead of **and**. It signals a slight **pause** between the **words or phrases** and helps the sentence to flow and not sound too jerky.

Use **and** to separate the **last two items** on a list.

The list should have been written:

Cutlass sword, flintlock pistol, treasure map, tricorn hat and compass.

SECTION 2: TO AVOID MISUNDERSTANDINGS

Commas

★ identify the person/ people being addressed.

★ make the sentence clearer and easier to read.

★ avoid any misunder- standings.

CAPTAIN MOODY'S RULES:

Commas are used to **separate the person/people** being identified **from the rest of the sentence**.

For example:

Make sure you bring a friend**,** Captain Moody.

Make sure you bring a friend Captain Moody.

BLACKBEARD'S WHINES:

Well shiver me timbers, that Captain Moody made me so confused! When he applied to be a pirate in my crew he wrote:

I like cooking dogs, reading and football.

My dog, Patch, was very worried!

PUNCTUA'S POINTS:

Commas are needed to make the meaning clear and avoid any terrible misunderstandings.
Captain Moody needs to think carefully when he makes lists.

For example:

I like cooking dogs, reading and football.

With **no comma to separate cooking from dogs**, this means that Captain Moody is talking **about cooking dogs**.

I like cooking, dogs, reading and football.

The **comma separates cooking from dogs**, so Captain Moody is **making a list** of the things he likes.

SECTION 3: TO SEPARATE PARTS OF A SENTENCE

Commas to separate parts of a sentence

Commas:

★ separate parts of a sentence to help make the meaning clear.

★ add extra information to the main part of a sentence.

CAPTAIN MOODY'S RULES:

A comma is used to:

★ **separate parts of a sentence** to help make the meaning clear.

★ **add extra information** to the **main message** of a sentence.

1. When joining two complete sentences, commas go:

   between the **first complete sentence** and the **conjunction** (and, but, so, or).

   Example:

   I saw a sea monster**, but** it didn't see me.

2. When adding extra information to a complete sentence, commas go:

   between the extra information and the main sentence.

3. The extra information often starts with conjunctions like:

   when, before, after, if, until, while, although

   Example:

   Before it saw me**,** I hid behind a rock.

BLACKBEARD'S WHINES:

Aye, me hearties!

Captain Moody made this mistake throughout his first draft and it made it difficult to understand his writing.

He wrote:

I saw a sea monster but it didn't see me.

Before it saw me I hid behind a rock.

PUNCTUA'S POINTS:

★ Too many short sentences can make your writing sound a bit jerky. They also slow the pace of the story because you keep having to stop all the time.

★ You can link your sentences and make them longer by:

  a. **joining two complete sentences** together. For example, using conjunctions like **but**.

  b. **adding extra information** to the **main part** of the sentence using conjunctions like **when**.

a. joining two sentences:

I saw a sea monster. It didn't see me.

These two complete sentences can be joined using **but**.

I saw a sea monster**, but** it didn't see me.

Note: there is a **comma before but** to link the two sentences.

b. adding extra information:

The reason Captain Moody wasn't eaten by the sea monster was **because** it didn't see him as he hid behind a rock, so he could link the sentences by writing:

When I saw a sea monster**, I** hid behind a rock**, so** it couldn't see me.

This time, Captain Moody is **adding some extra information** to the main message to make it clear why he wasn't seen by the sea monster.

Main message – The sea monster didn't see me.

Extra information explaining why – I hid behind a rock.

So it couldn't see me doesn't make sense on its own. To make sense, it needs to be linked to the main message by a comma.

Note:

i. the conjunction **when** at the beginning

ii. the **comma after** the extra information

Tip: look out for the following **conjunctions** that help add more detail to your writing.

When, before, after, if, until, although

Appendix

Captain Moody's editing checklist level 1: punctuation

Captain Moody's editing checklist level 2: punctuation

Blackbeard's challenge

Certificate: editing level 1

Certificate: editing level 2

CAPTAIN MOODY'S EDITING CHECKLIST LEVEL 1: PUNCTUATION

		I confirm when I am editing, I check that:	✓
A.		**Sentences**	
1.		My sentences make sense.	
2.		My sentences end with a full stop.	
B.		**Capital letters**	
3.		My sentences start with a capital letter.	
4.		'I' has a capital letter.	
5.		Names of people and places have a capital letter.	
6.		Names of days and months have a capital letter.	
C.		**Questions and exclamations**	
7.		I put a question mark at the end of a direct question.	
8.		I put an exclamation mark to signal a surprise or outburst.	
D.		**Speech**	
9.		I put speech marks around the words being spoken.	
10.		I started a new line when the person speaking changes.	
11.		I started the speech with a capital letter.	
		Signature: Date:	

	CAPTAIN MOODY'S EDITING CHECKLIST LEVEL 2: PUNCTUATION	
	I confirm when I am editing, I check that:	✓
A.	**Sentences**	
1.	My sentences are clear and easy to read.	
2.	I used a full stop, question mark or exclamation mark at the end of my sentences.	
B.	**Capital letters**	
3.	I used capital letters for 'I,' names of people, places, days and months.	
C.	**Apostrophes**	
4.	I used an apostrophe where something belongs to someone.	
5.	I used an apostrophe where letters are missing.	
6.	I haven't mixed up it's/its or they're/their/there.	
D.	**Commas**	
7.	I have used a comma to identify the person/people being addressed.	
8.	I have used commas to separate items in a list.	
9.	I have used commas to separate extra information from the main part of a sentence.	
	Signature: Date:	

BLACKBEARD'S CHALLENGE

Correct the errors:

Have you been paying attention? Do you remember the mistakes I picked out and had to correct in Captain Moody's first draft? Test your knowledge by completing my challenge. (*You can always look back to check if you are not sure.*)

1. **Correct the passage so that it makes sense**

   i sailed across the sea i was with my pirate crew, we saw an island i thought i could see a monster when we got closer i saw it was an island of monsters

2. **Spot the comma splicing**

   i.   Read the passage aloud.

   ii. Make a mark for each unit of sense.

   iii. Insert a full stop.

   a.   Sunlight beamed through the leaves of the palm trees, something was up there, beady eyes peered down at me.

   b.   The map was in the bottle, curled up in a scroll, I stuck my fingers in to get it out.

3. **Capital letters**

   Look for 'I,' names of people, places, days and months and insert a capital letter.

   a.   The island had the volcano of death, the forest of doom, the swamp of stink, the river of evil, the waterfall of terror, the lake of madness and the cave of monsters.

   b.   Captain Moody said, "i will set sail on saturday."

   c.   i keep looking for blackbeard, but i haven't seen him since july.

4. **Question marks – yes or no?**

   Insert either **a question mark** or **a full stop** at the end of these sentences:

   a.   Where is the treasure

   b.   Blackbeard asked to look at the map

   c.   Why don't raise the flag now

   d.   The crew asked me why I never listen to them

   e.   The monster asked me why I am so mean

   f.   Could you show me your pirate ship

5. Exclamation marks

When would you use an exclamation mark?

a. I like going fishing

b. I hate pirates

6. Punctuate the speech

a. Shiver me timbers I yelled.

b. Where is the treasure I asked.

c. Over there I said happily. We can set sail straight away.

d. I really should have brought my sword I moaned. By now, I could see the monster getting closer. I want my mummy I cried. My legs began to shake and my bottom lip wobbled.

7. Apostrophes

i. *Insert the apostrophe in the correct place.*

ii. *Check its/it's and their/they're/there.*

a. The cannon and cannonballs from the Captains ship are ready to load. I cant lift them though theyre too heavy.

b. Ive been searching for the monster but I cant see it anywhere. I dont know where to look next. Its missing.

c. There is the treasure. Its inside the cave over theyre.

8. Commas in a list

i. Insert commas to separate the items on the list.

ii. Explore what would happen if you put the commas in the wrong place.

I boarded the ship and saw the ship's wheel cannonballs ropes cannons and a figurehead.

9. Identifying the people being addressed

Read sentences a, b and c, and discuss questions 1–3 with a partner.

a. If you have your weapons then we can prepare Captain.

b. I'm hungry. Let's eat Blackbeard.

c. Cut the ropes Captain we need to set sail.

Questions:

1. What do these sentences mean?
2. Where should the comma go?
3. How does inserting a comma change the meaning?

Certificate

EDITING LEVEL 1

awarded to

Name:

In recognition of your hard work in editing your writing.

Captain Moody & Punctua

Date

Certificate

EDITING LEVEL 2

awarded to

Name:

In recognition of your hard work in editing your writing.

Captain Moody & Punctua

Date